WILTSHIRE

A portrait in colour

BILL MEADOWS & NIGEL VILE

COUNTRYSIDE BOOKS
NEWBURY, BERKSHIRE

First published 2003
© Photographs, Bill Meadows 2003
© Text, Nigel Vile 2003

COUNTRYSIDE BOOKS
3 Catherine Road
Newbury, Berkshire

To view our complete range of books,
please visit us at
www.countrysidebooks.co.uk

ISBN 1 85306 798 9

front Cover - Vale of Pewsey from Tan Hill Way
Back Cover - Fishing on River Avon, Salisbury.

Photo on page 1 is of the Ridgeway
Photo on page 4 is of the bluebell woods, near Oare
Photo on page 5 is of Marlborough
Photo on page 12, courtesy of Honda UK Ltd.
Photo on page 22, courtesy of Nicholas Battle
Photo on page 80 shows Salisbury Plain near Chitterne

Designed by Peter Davies, Nautilus Design
Produced through MRM Associates Ltd., Reading
Printed in Italy

CONTENTS

INTRODUCTION

Wiltshire is one of England's hidden gems. Many people tend to rush through it on their way south, lured by the sea and sand on offer in Dorset, Devon and Cornwall. They are missing a treat, though, for Wiltshire has magic, mystery, peace and solitude. It also has some of the finest scenery in southern England.

The expression 'as different as chalk and cheese' describes Wiltshire perfectly, for here are two distinct landscapes. Firstly, there is the chalk downland rising to almost 1,000 ft above sea level at Tan Hill, east of Devizes. This is perhaps the county's most well known natural feature and provides a dramatic backdrop for some of the ancient archaeological sites scattered around Wiltshire. Apart from majestic Stonehenge, there is the vast stone circle at Avebury, West Kennet with its intriguing long barrow, the Iron Age hill fort of Old Sarum and the handsome white horses that adorn the hillsides at Westbury and Cherhill.

Below these chalk hills, lie the clay vales through which rivers such as the Wylye, the Kennet and the Avon flow. This rich dairy and arable land led to a thriving agricultural economy from which picturesque market towns such as Devizes and Wootton Bassett still thrive.

Salisbury, in the south of the county, with its imposing cathedral, is as fine a city as can be found anywhere, and retains many of its imposing old buildings. Whilst in the north, Swindon, once an important railway town, now forms the hub of modern Wiltshire, with its striking business parks, its excellent shopping malls and its popular leisure parks.

With the help of some superb images from landscape photographer Bill Meadows, I commend this book to you as a perfect introduction to one of the country's most ancient and glorious landscapes. I hope it will spur you to spend some time discovering its delights.

Nigel Vile

CRICKLADE

*'I passed through that villainous hole Cricklade about two hours ago, and
certainly a more rascally place I never set me eyes on.'*

WILLIAM COBBETT (1821)

It is difficult to understand why Cobbett found the ancient borough of Cricklade to be such a disagreeable place. Close to the source of the River Thames, Cricklade (*opposite*) can boast a rich historic and archaeological heritage, which includes its fortified Saxon town walls and two contrasting churches in St Mary's and St Sampson's. There is also the handsome main street lined with many 17th and 18th-century buildings, as well as the ancient market cross and a clock erected in 1897 to commemorate Queen Victoria's Jubilee.

The town, like so many other historic settlements, can trace its origins back to its geographical location. Several small streams merge with the River Thames in the vicinity, forming a natural flood plain which often led to impassable conditions in the winter months. It was not until the arrival of the Romans that a permanent crossing was constructed over these waterways – a raised causeway was erected to carry Ermin Street across the flood plain. The settlement that grew up to the south of this route

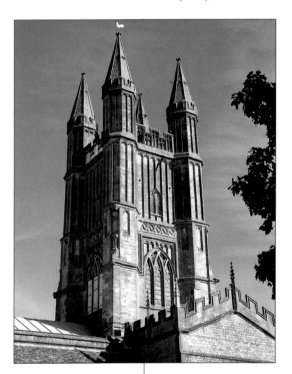

running from Silchester to Gloucester became the town of Cricklade.

Communications have always been the key to the town's prosperity, starting with the navigable Thames, and continuing with the Thames & Severn Canal and the Midland & South West Junction Railway, through to today's A419. The canal arrived in 1789, and Cricklade soon became a waterways junction with the construction of the North Wiltshire Canal to Swindon. To this day, a former agent's house and warehouse stand at the canal junction, although much of the waterway itself has disappeared.

St Sampson's church, whose tall pinnacled tower (*inset*) is a prominent landmark across these upper reaches of the Thames Valley, has arguably the finest stained-glass window of any parish church in the county. Designed by Charles Kempe in 1888, it shows Christ in majesty, together with the beautifully interpreted figures of eight saints. Prominent among these 'Men of God' is St Sampson himself, ginger-bearded and carrying a large model of his church.

ASHTON KEYNES

*'I had to go through a village called Ashton Keines with which place I was very much smitten.
It is now a straggling village but to a certainty it has been a large Market Town.'*

WILLIAM COBBETT, *Rural Rides* (1826)

Were a film company looking for a rural idyll in which to base a film centred on the English landscape, Ashton Keynes would come near the top of any list. One traveller noted that the village had a beehive in a back garden, a black cat asleep on a doormat, a memorial seat presented by the WI and ducks waddling down the main street. It is that sort of place.

Each house appears to have its own drawbridge crossing the local stream, which householders proudly boast is none other than the infant River Thames. Look on the O.S. sheets, however, and the real Thames can be seen meandering across the meadows to the south of the village. What flows through Ashton Keynes is too neat and orderly to be the real thing, it is a branch routed through the village in centuries past to feed some ancient mill, not a fact the local estate agents are keen to point out.

As with so many villages in the Cotswolds, social change has made Ashton Keynes a virtually unrecognisable place to the older generations. In 1851, in the 35 homes in Gosditch Street, there lived a tailor, saddler, tallow chandler, stonemason, many glove makers and a cobbler. The Horse and Jockey Inn was little more than a 'scrumpy house', selling cider made from apples from local orchards.

The three ancient crosses in the centre of the village, each with steps and virtually intact shafts, are indicative of its former commercial importance, whilst round about lie any number of stone cottages and houses set within a conservation area. It is little wonder that Cobbett was 'very much smitten' with Ashton Keynes.

MALMESBURY

'There is a right fair and costely piece of worke in the Market-place made al of stone, and curiously voutid for poore market folkes to stande dry when rayne cummith'

JOHN LELAND (1506-1552)

Driving into Malmesbury (*opposite*), the signs at the entrance to the town proudly announce to visitors that this is England's oldest borough, Athelstan granting this hilltop settlement its first charter as far back as 924 AD. Dominating the town is the ancient abbey (*inset*), founded by St Aldhelm, whose outline provides a distinct landmark in this north-west corner of the county. Despite its somewhat ruinous

state, due to the collapse of the great crossing tower and spire in the 15th century, Malmesbury Abbey remains an atmospheric and hauntingly beautiful place of worship.

Architecturally, it is a pleasing blend of flying buttresses and vaulting, decorative motifs and grand arches. What catches the eye of most visitors, however, is the massive, intricately carved Late Norman south porch. A plain outer arch shelters the Norman arch of eight continuous orders, prompting Pevsner to describe this masterwork as the *chef d'oeuvre* of Malmesbury.

Much of the town's wealth can be traced back to the medieval textile trade that was of such importance in the West of England. It was from this period that the town's market cross can be dated, a beautiful structure comprising eight open arches, rising above which are a series of battlements and carved figures, sited beneath trefoil-headed canopies. What a grand structure to merely keep the poor market folk dry!

Ultimately, however, it is the people that make a place as much as the physical constructions that line its streets and byways. One of the great characters in Malmesbury's history was a monk named Elmer. Determined to defy the laws of gravity, he equipped himself with a pair of wings and leapt from one of the abbey's towers. Initial elation at gliding for over 200 yards was somewhat tempered when he fell from a great height, breaking both legs.

SWINDON

'Swindon is steeped in history, with some wonderful Victorian architecture and gorgeous countryside.'

JONATHON GLANCEY, *Guardian* Architect and Design Critic

The past fifty years have seen Swindon virtually reinvent itself. From a traditional working-class railway town, it has become one of the major centres of technology-based industry and commerce along the M4 corridor. From an archetypal 'one-horse town', where life revolved around daily shift patterns at the Great Western Railway's workshops, the local economy has diversified into areas such as banking, insurance and distribution, mirroring the changes that have occurred throughout the national economy over the same period.

Dominating the town is the former David Murray John Building, now known as the Brunel Tower. Murray John, the local politician known as 'Mr Swindon', grew up in Huddersfield in the 1930s. Having seen the problems inherent in a town when its main employer went into decline, he was determined that the same fate should not befall his adopted home town.

One of the more incongruous sights greeting visitors arriving via the motorway is a traditional windmill standing amidst the modern glass-fronted office blocks of the Windmill Hill Business Park (*inset*). Despite the name, this was never the historic site of an actual windmill. The mill only arrived in the 1980s, moved brick by brick from its original location in nearby Chiseldon, where it had stood since the 1820s.

At the end of the day, though, Swindon is not content to be yet another English museum piece. Business continues to grow at a fast rate, with investment and employment well above the national average. The local economy is modern and diversified, with its lifeline being the M4 motorway linking the commercial centres of Bristol and London. As the town's publicity literature boasts, Swindon can offer 'excellent communications that provide a competitive business environment without equal in the UK'.

SWINDON – HONDA

'I'd never seen anything quite like this before. The speed at which everything works is quite amazing.'

JACQUES VILLENEUVE, Formula 1 driver – On a visit to Honda Swindon, 2002

Japan and Wiltshire do not immediately spring to mind as natural partners. On the one hand, a bright, modern economy, completely rebuilt since the Second World War, and on the other, an ancient landscape, famous for its stone circles and hill forts, round barrows and tumuli. This notwithstanding, when Jacques Villeneuve visited Honda Swindon (*inset*) in June 2002, his visit coincided with the production of the half-millionth Swindon-built Civic.

To become a recognised world-class company, Honda needed a European base and Swindon welcomed the Japanese with open arms. The town had much to offer: firstly, there were the people, with engineering in their blood, following the town's historic association with the Great Western Railway; secondly the excellent communications, with the M4 motorway (*opposite*) and other trunk routes giving easy access to both Heathrow airport and the South Coast ports; and finally, there was a greenfield site at South Marston, a former airfield stretching to some 370 acres.

September 2001 saw Honda open a second car plant in the town, with new manufacturing systems bringing even greater levels of flexibility, speed and efficiency. This was the first 'green field' car plant to be built in Britain for over eight years, giving Honda the capacity to produce 250,000 cars each year. The new plant uses some of the world's most advanced production systems, distilled from manufacturing know-how in Japan, North America and the UK. The 'New Manufacturing System' replaces model specific equipment and production processes with those which are universal – ancient and modern meet in Wiltshire!

October 2002 marked the tenth anniversary of Honda's arrival in the town, the company initially forging a partnership with Rover who also had an operational plant in Swindon. Over £1.15 billion has been invested in the company's Wiltshire operations, and it comes as no surprise to hear Honda President Hiroyki Yoshino state 'the UK is a great place to build cars – Swindon is a key element'.

THE RAILWAYS

'Jeremy Clarkson profiles the engineer Isambard Kingdom Brunel whose Great Western Railway slashed the journey time between Paddington and Bristol; an achievement matched only by Railtrack's success in lengthening it again more than 150 years later.'

Venue *magazine TV choice comment (October 2002)*

The GWR was completed in three years after the initial section from Paddington to Maidenhead was opened in 1841. 'God's Wonderful Railway' to generations of travellers, the GWR is memorable as the longest surviving Victorian railway company, being 114 years old on its nationalisation in 1947. Daniel Gooch, the company's Superintendent of Locomotives, established the Swindon Workshop in the 1840s. Located at the junction with the Cheltenham and Great Western Union Railway, as many as 14,000 men were employed in the works at its peak.

Along its length, nothing can rival Box Tunnel (*opposite*) between Chippenham and Bath. Nearly 2 miles in length, its construction used only hand labour and horses turning rope-drums for haulage. During the last six months of its construction, 4,000 men and 300 horses worked around the clock, in two 12-hour shifts, in order to complete the contract on time. More than 100 men were killed in the course of the work and many more injured, statistics visitors to its grand western portal would do well to ponder.

The Great Western Railway is now but a memory, despite its modern re-incarnation in the form of First Great Western, one of Britain's privatised railway companies. Swindon's workshops, however, remain as a testimony to this former era. Recently restored, the former workshops now house the GWR Museum (*inset*), a tribute to this once great railway company. An active workshop, a reconstructed station platform, a restored railway worker's cottage and a whole host of other railway memorabilia bring to life an age long gone but seldom forgotten amongst railway enthusiasts.

WOOTTON BASSETT AND LYDIARD PARK

'Wootton Bassett is a friendly thriving community'

THE TOWN GUIDE

When Swindon was little more than a hilltop village, Wootton Bassett was a thriving market town for this corner of Wiltshire. Dominating the lengthy High Street is the old town hall (*opposite*), a

timbered building dating from 1700. A 'hall for all seasons', the town hall did not always look as it does today. The original plan was for an upper room or council chamber built on 15 pillars, whilst at ground level there was to be a store room for market commodities, as well as a lock-up where drunkards could be sobered up!

Drink appears to have played no small part in the history of the town. There is a tale of one drunk who was brought before the town mayor after an overnight drinking session. When asked for a confession of guilt, the man replied, 'You knows your worship was just as drunk as I was.' The mayor, who had clearly attended the same watering hole, replied, 'That was different. Now I am the mayor and I am going to fine you five shillings.'

In nearby Lydiard Park stands a neo-Palladian Georgian mansion (*inset*). The present house dates from 1743, when a medieval mansion was remodelled by the 2nd Viscount St John, half-brother of Lord Bolingbroke, the well-known Tory politician. The St John family first came to the area in the 15th century, with the estate remaining in their hands until 1943, when financial problems led them to sell the house and its grounds to Swindon Corporation.

The mansion contains a number of state rooms, including a ballroom, where the rococo ceiling appears to catch the eye of the guidebook writers, as well as Georgian furniture and a collection of family portraits. The grounds are equally attractive, with oaks, beeches and cedars surrounding an impressive lake, with the rolling lawns being typical of the late 18th-century country estate. It is altogether a fine public amenity for the citizens of Swindon to enjoy.

THE RIDGEWAY

'By definition there can be no records of prehistoric tracks so one can merely surmise that the Ridgeway . . . forms the oldest road in Britain.'

GEOFFREY WRIGHT, *Roads and Trackways of Wessex* (1988)

As a keen walker, the Ridgeway is one of my favourite walking destinations in the county. Not on some glorious summer weekend, when this ancient trackway is awash with people but rather on a gloomy weekday morning in mid-winter, with an intermittent mist enveloping the chalk downlands across which the ancients carved this historic route.

For at least 5,000 years, people – be they drovers, traders or contemporary ramblers – have walked or ridden the Ridgeway. This is part of one vast prehistoric track that once stretched for 250 miles from the Dorset coast to the Wash in Norfolk. It provided a route over the high ground for travellers, keen to escape the wooded vales below, with their spring line villages and consequent dampness.

Along its line, the ancients left their mark. New Stone Age men, the first farmers in Britain, constructed their long barrows; the Bronze Age peoples dragged the huge sarsen stones from the surrounding downland to create the magnificent stone circle at Avebury, as well as groups of round barrows along the line of the Ridgeway; the Iron Age tribes constructed those vast hillforts, such as Barbury Castle, through whose ramparts the Ridgeway literally cuts its course.

With so much mystery and intrigue along its way, it is little wonder that this ancient route attracts mystics from across the globe and possibly from further afield. In the arable land that lies alongside it, recent summers have seen a proliferation of crop circles. Long may these circles hold their secrets, and not fall prey to the seemingly all embracing scientific rationalism.

CASTLE COMBE

'One of the delights of visiting villages, be it here in Wiltshire, other areas of England or continental Europe, is discovering the characteristics and peculiarities that make each one unique.'

BRIAN J. WOODRUFFE, *Wiltshire Villages* (1982)

Wiltshire simply abounds in what the guidebooks refer to as the 'traditional English village'. Castle Combe nestling in a wooded valley, watered by a sparkling Cotswold stream, displays all the archetypal features that would bring a lump to the throat of many an English expatriate. Stone cottages, village greens, ancient churches and hostelries – these features are so commonplace that the locals do become rather blasé about what lies quite literally on their doorstep. It was only when accompanying some German friends into Castle Combe that I fully appreciated just how beautiful this place really is – they simply gazed in awe, almost speechless at what has been voted 'the prettiest village in England'.

Castle Combe is a rather special place. The view from the ancient bridge across the By Brook, up the main street lined with cottages of mellow limestone to the Market Cross is truly memorable. If it creates a sense of déjà vu, it is because this is the view that appears on any number of calendars, greetings cards, chocolate boxes and biscuit tins. The familiarity of Castle Combe might also be due to its starring role in the 1966 version of *The Story of Dr Doolittle*, when the village was turned into a fishing harbour, with attractive boats moored along the local river.

ALDBOURNE AND RAMSBURY

'The independent spirit of the village . . . springs perhaps from its compact form, the village being built in the main around the Green and the Square which nestle at the junction of the valleys.'

THE ALDBOURNE VILLAGE WEB SITE (2002)

Back in 1998, Trowbridge Town – my local senior football side – went bankrupt. One year later, the club was resurrected and began to ply its trade in the Wiltshire League. No longer were the supporters heading across country to towns and cities such as Gloucester or Cheltenham, Dover or Chelmsford – rather it was afternoons out in such idyllic rural locations as Shrewton and Biddestone, Pewsey and Aldbourne.

Aldbourne became the supporters' favourite destination, and what a shock it must have been when a coachload of well-behaved but noisy fans arrived in this most genteel of Wiltshire villages! Located within the chalky folds of the Marlborough Downs, Aldbourne (*opposite*) is arranged around a village green, the scene completed with brick and flint houses, a fine hostelry and a church with a quite exceptional Perpendicular tower.

In the 17th and 18th centuries, Aldbourne was famous for its bell foundry, with bells for animals – particularly horses – being its speciality. Willow-plaiting and straw-plaiting were also found in the village, the willow being used for summer decoration of fireplaces, with the straw being used in the millinery trade.

In the Kennet Valley, a few miles south of Aldbourne lies the large village of Ramsbury (*inset*). The main street, with its pleasing miscellany of shops and houses, broadens near the Bell Inn, in front of which once stood the famous Ramsbury elm. The victim of Dutch Elm Disease, the original tree was a seedling in the time of King Charles I, with John Wesley preaching beneath its boughs nearly 130 years later. In 1986, a semi-mature oak tree was planted to replace the elm, an event of such monument that it made the BBC national news broadcasts.

CHIPPENHAM AND BIDDESTONE

'From the Golden Gate we descend rapidly towards Chippenham, our last town on the road.'

CECIL ROBERTS, *And so to Bath* (1940)

As a youngster, I remember Chippenham being little more than a sleepy Wiltshire market town, on the main railway line from Bristol to London. Friday was market day, and farmers from far and wide would congregate in the market at the top of Station Hill. Many years later, I picked up a national newspaper that was running a story under the headline, 'Chippenham – fastest growing town in Europe'. This was in the early 1980s, since when the town's growth has continued unabated. It is communications that have been the magnet – easy access to the M4 motorway, and fast railway links to Bath and Bristol, Swindon and London. Chippenham has indeed become the archetypal dormitory town.

Penetrate the town's ring roads and their numerous roundabouts, however, and it is still possible to discover something of the old Chippenham (*inset*). The ancient streets, especially St Mary's Street running alongside the parish church, offer a medley of buildings. There are half-timbered houses from the 16th and 17th centuries, as well as gabled and stately Georgian properties. From the medieval church – with its octagonal spire surmounting a tower with a balustraded parapet – the bustling and modern high street runs downhill to the River Avon.

A few miles west of Chippenham, lies the delightful village of Biddestone (*opposite*) whose village green is perhaps the most photogenic in the county. Here we find a genuine duck pond supporting – as Brian Woodruffe points out in his book, *Wiltshire Villages* – a *'veritable paddling of ducks and their domesticated variants'*. Surrounding the green is a number of well-tended 18th-century cottages and elegant houses, the setting completed by the White Horse Inn. Standing somewhat apart from the village centre is St Nicholas church, with its unusual 13th-century stone bell turret and a plain – but not unappealing – Norman doorway.

CORSHAM

'A walk down Corsham's High Street cannot be hurried.'

CECIL ROBERTS, *And so to Bath* (1940)

The main London Road runs to the north of Corsham, through Pickwick, in fact. In 1835, Charles Dickens, then a young reporter, did pass this way en route to Bath to report on a political speech. Possibly the name was embedded on his subconscience, to appear later in the title of that famous work, possibly the name was picked up from Moses Pickwick, a Bath coach proprietor. Whatever the story, the passing traffic on what is now known less romantically as the A4 really does itself a disservice in bypassing Corsham.

Many of the fine buildings that line the High Street date from the 17th and 18th centuries. There are the grand Georgian houses standing cheek by jowl alongside the ranks of Flemish weavers' cottages, with their neatly gabled bay windows. The Hungerford Almshouses, dating from 1668, are a delight to the eye, as is the town hall (*inset*), erected in the 1780s. Follow Church Street and, as well as discovering a most unexpected folly in the form of a ruinous castle, you may well stumble across the grave of Sarah Jarvis in the churchyard. Nothing unusual in that, perhaps, apart from the fact that she died in 1753, aged 107!

The jewel in the crown, however, is Corsham Court (*opposite*), home to the Methuen family since 1745. Having made their fortune from the local woollen trade, the Methuens proceeded to remodel the northern frontage of the grand house along Palladian lines, as well as employing none other than 'Capability' Brown to lay out the landscaped gardens and parkland.

Corsham Court contains arguably one of the finest private collections of Old Masters, as well as an excellent collection of English furniture that includes both Chippendale and Robert Adam. Most visitors, however, come away with memories of the fine architecture, the gables and mullioned windows, the pediments and

pinnacles that break the skyline from every angle. No wonder Cecil Roberts thought Corsham a place that could not be hurried.

LACOCK

'Lacock is easily the most remarkable and the most beautiful village in all Wiltshire.'

EDWARD HUTTON, *Highways and Byways in Wiltshire* (1917)

All too often, the regional tourist boards flatter to deceive. Flowery prose and deceptive photography are used to present an image of a town or city, an attraction or an historic monument, which ultimately disappoints. With the charming village of Lacock, however, no amount of hype or publicity could do justice to what is – without a shadow of doubt – the most beautiful village in Wiltshire.

The settlement, formerly a major wool producing centre, is based around four streets – Church Street, West Street, East Street and the High Street – and still very much resembles a medieval town. Lacock's attractive houses (*inset*) cover every century from the 13th to the 18th, with little recent development to spoil the overall effect. The pleasing blend of styles is reflected in the building materials used in the village – everything from timber-frames to brick and stone. Sharp gables and decorated overhangs, projecting eaves and dormer windows combine to produce a perfect mix of architectural styles.

What attracts most visitors to Lacock, though, is the fine abbey (*opposite*). Founded in 1232, and converted into a country house after 1539, Lacock Abbey can boast not only medieval cloisters, a sacristy and a chapter house, but also a 16th-century stable court, fine towers and chimneys and a Gothic hall dating from 1754. The abbey was the home of the Talbot family, who left their whole estate – including the village – to the National Trust.

William Henry Fox Talbot (1800-77) was one of the great pioneers of photography. His negative of an oriel window in the abbey is the oldest negative in existence, and many other early photographic studies of his home can be seen in the Fox Talbot Museum, housed in a traditional barn alongside the abbey gates. Somehow it seems wholly appropriate that the roots of photography can be traced back to this most photogenic of villages.

CALNE

'Calne stands dreaming in its valley amid the hills.'

TOWN GUIDE, 1950

Calne lies on the main A4 road which, prior to the opening of the M4 motorway, was the trunk road from Bristol to London. In the era of horse and carriage, the town was a coaching stop on the London Road, with inns such as the Lansdowne Arms standing as testimony to this period in Calne's history. It was this same London Road that was responsible for arguably the biggest single development in the town's history, way back in the 19th century.

At the time, Irish pigs were imported into Bristol before being quite literally herded to London. Two brothers – C&T Harris – decided to establish a bacon business in Calne, buying in some of the passing pigs as raw material. The business diversified into pies and sausages, but sadly fell victim to cheap imported meat in the late 1970s. The demolition of the five-storey factory left a gaping hole in the town's economy, a void that took many years to fill. A lasting reminder of this once thriving business is a delightful sculpture (*inset*).

Head out of town on the London Road and it is not long before the Marlborough Downs appear on the horizon, dominated by the Cherhill White Horse. A Doctor Christopher Alsop, whose efforts earned him the nickname of the 'mad doctor', cut this magnificent hill figure in 1780. The appendage 'mad' was the result of his construction methods – he would stand up to a mile from the hillside with a primitive megaphone, shouting out instructions to his men who would mark out the figure's outline using white flags.

Alongside the Cherhill White Horse is the Lansdowne Monument, a fine obelisk which the 3rd Marquis of Lansdowne erected in the middle of the 19th-century to commemorate his ancestor Sir William Petty, an economist from the Classical School. Erected above the highest point on the Great West Road, the monument towers some 125 ft above the hilltop and can be seen from up to 30 miles away.

TWO GRAND DESIGNS

'All that makes life worth living is at lovely Bowood'

THOMAS MOORE (1779-1852)

Less well known than the Bloomsbury Set, the Bowood Circle could boast such luminaries as Richard Price and Joseph Priestley, Jeremy Bentham and Thomas Moore amongst their number. The Earl of Shelburne – latterly known as the 1st Marquis of Lansdowne – was a

patron of art, science and letters, and enjoyed nothing more than entertaining the great literary figures of the day.

The Earl purchased Bowood Park in 1754, commissioning the architect Henry Keene to complete an unfinished early Georgian house on the estate that lay between Calne and Chippenham. The result was a mansion in the Italian style (*inset*), ornamented by a grand Doric portico, with an annex 300 ft long, a copy of a wing of Diocletian's palace at Spalato. The genius that was 'Capability' Brown completed the setting, with gently sloping lawns stretching away from the terraced rose gardens to a graceful lake below the house.

Wilton House (*opposite*), in the south of the county, is another of the great treasures of England, and home to the Earls of Pembroke for nearly five centuries. Back in the 9th century, this was the site of a nunnery founded by King Alfred. The nunnery was replaced by a Benedictine abbey in the 12th century, with the property and its surrounding lands being surrendered at the time of the Dissolution to Henry VIII. A large Tudor home was then built on the land, incorporating parts of the old abbey walls, with the current Palladian-style building – attributed to Inigo Jones – dating from the 17th century.

Around Wilton House lie acres of extensive parkland, bordered by the River Nadder. The setting is completed by a Palladian bridge, a Millennium water feature, the *Whispering Seat* and the *Rose and Water Garden*. Huge stately cedars rise from the lawns of the great house, emphasising its rich historic associations. Indeed, it is even alleged that Shakespeare gave his first performance of *Twelfth Night* here at Wilton.

AVEBURY

'Avebury is a haunting place to see at all times and in all weathers . . .'

SIR JOHN BETJEMAN (1950)

Although very much in the shadow of Stonehenge, the stone circle at Avebury can boast an even more impressive set of statistics. This is the largest prehistoric stone circle in the world, with its surrounding ramparts enclosing a site of some 28 acres. This massive embankment rises to a height of 18 ft, before swooping into an 11 ft ditch, whilst the walk around the complete circle extends for close on one mile.

The vast stones, the largest of which weighs well over 50 tons, are sarsen stones, hard sandstone blocks that lay scattered across the nearby Marlborough Downs. Geologists describe these sarsens as 'remnants of a siliceous duricrust layer', whilst the locals have traditionally referred to them as 'Grey Wethers' on account of their resembling flocks of sheep when lying scattered across the local landscape.

The original 180 stones were brought to Avebury around 2,400 BC, and arranged into a large circle that enclosed two smaller circles, one of which contained another smaller ring – the intricacies of design were not lost on our prehistoric ancestors. Today, just 49 of the stones remain, with many of the original boulders having been broken up in medieval times on account of their pagan origins. Suffice to say, a good deal of this vandalised stone ended up as building material in the local cottages!

Avebury can also offer the visitor attractive cottages of thatch and

brick, a characterful church – built outside of the pagan circle, the Alexander Keiller Museum with its archaeological displays and a 17th-century barn that houses a museum of rural life (*inset*). With a fine manor house, the Red Lion Inn and a National Trust emporium, the village has so much to offer.

SILBURY HILL AND WEST KENNETT LONG BARROW

'A great mound soon looms up on our right. It is Silbury Hill and, like Avebury, it is a mystery.'

CECIL ROBERTS, *And So to Bath* (1940)

That this part of Wiltshire is important countryside for the archaeologist is evident from the fact that both of these ancient monuments have warranted a reference in the *Guinness Book of Records*. With no cranes or engineering apparatus, with no shovels even - for they dug with antlers and oxen shoulder-blades - our prehistoric ancestors somehow contrived to construct an earthwork that covers 5 acres and is 300 ft around at its summit. These vast dimensions constitute the largest artificial mound in Europe, whose size can be gauged by the fact that Silbury Hill (*opposite*) would just fit within the confines of Trafalgar Square. As with so many of the mysterious landmarks in the county, its actual role or purpose remains lost in the sands of time. Generations of archaeologists have sought to unravel the meaning of Silbury Hill, but all to no avail.

The *Guinness Book of Records* also claims that West Kennett Long Barrow (*inset*) is 'England's longest barrow containing a megalithic chamber'. It certainly is an impressive ancient monument that stands – to quote the 18th-century historian William Stukeley – 'east and west, pointing to the dragon's head on Overton Hill'. This is a reference to the shape of a 'great stone serpent' formed on the landscape by a series of historic landmarks in and around Avebury. Consisting originally of a trapezoid mound 330 ft long, formed of a core of sarsen boulders and a capping of chalk rubble from adjoining ditches, a stand of vertical stone uprights rise sentry-like at the entrance to the tomb. Upwards of 40 individuals had their earthly remains laid to rest on this remote Wiltshire hilltop, with excavations in the 1950s also unearthing pottery shards, flint implements and beads. West Kennett Long Barrow is a truly magical relic standing in what is the most mysterious corner of the county.

MARLBOROUGH

'Marlborough is one spectacularly long and wide High Street running parallel to the River Kennet.'

Nikolaus Pevsner, *The Buildings of England: Wiltshire* (1963)

Pevsner's description may be brief and to the point, but it summarises perfectly the impression that this most attractive of Wiltshire settlements leaves on the visitor. Marlborough is a warm and dignified downland market town (*inset*), consisting in the main of one broad long street of handsome buildings, teashops, antique and gift shops. Visit the town on a Saturday, and a good number of market stalls line the centre of the High Street, whilst once a year the broad thoroughfare is closed to traffic for the annual Mop Fair.

The town's most learned institution is Marlborough College, located at the western end of the High Street. This was formerly a fine mansion built by Francis, Lord Seymour, whilst later it was the Castle Inn, a famous haunt on the coaching route from London to the West Country. The Castle enjoyed great popularity in its heyday, entertaining such notables as Pepys, Sheridan and Lord Chatham, who arrived with his gout and a vast train of servants!

The college grounds house the site of Marlborough Castle, as well as the ancient 'Castle Mound'. This is said to be the grave of Merlin *Maerl's Barrow* – from which Marlborough gets its name. Legend holds that Merlin is lying here sleeping until that occasion when Britain is next in need of his services. These facts are recorded on the town's crest, with its representation of the Castle Mound and a Latin motto that translates 'to the bones of the wise Merlin'.

Heading east from the town, the London road passes through Savernake Forest (*opposite*) whose 2,300 acres stretch across an undulating plateau above Marlborough. Prior to the Conquest, the forest embraced a much larger slice of the Wiltshire countryside, and was a noted royal hunting ground. To this day, herds of roe and fallow deer still roam the deeper parts of the forest.

THE VALE OF PEWSEY

*'I am just returned from the top of Old Adam, having thought of you as I can scarce help
doing always on those green sloping Downs, with all that wide country spread below.'*

MARIA HARE (1831)

Adam's Grave, a late Neolithic long barrow, sits proudly on the North Wessex Downs overlooking the Vale of Pewsey (*inset*). Described as 'my land of promise' by William Cobbett, this clay vale stretches for little more than 10 miles from Devizes through to Pewsey

itself. What makes the vale so special, however, is its setting against a backdrop of some of the finest downland in the county.

These North Wessex Downs, much of which still consist of unimproved grassland, rise to some 964 ft above sea-level at Tan Hill, the highest point in Wiltshire. Tan Hill is a corruption of St Anne's Hill, and was the site of an annual fair held on St Anne's Day – 26th July – each year. The main business of the day was trade in livestock, in particular sheep, although as a social gathering in the local agricultural calendar, the fair must have been some occasion.

Carved on the south-facing scarp is the Alton Barnes White Horse, allegedly visible from Old Sarum near Salisbury, some 20 miles distant. It was cut in 1812, at the expense of a Mr Robert Pile of Alton Barnes, who paid a journeyman painter £20 to execute the task. John Thorpe, nicknamed 'Jack the Painter', was foolishly paid in advance and promptly disappeared! He was later hanged for some crime that history has not recorded, leaving Pile the task of completing the horse himself. Such is the stuff of legends!

Running the length of these downland hilltops is the Wansdyke, a linear frontier of bank-and-ditch built around the 6th century by the Britons, to act as a defence against invading pagan Saxons. Walking the course of the Wansdyke high on these hills has been described as 'one of the most spectacular experiences in British field archaeology'.

GREAT BEDWYN

'Some experts believe that Bedwyn is named after the Clematis. Bedwine, or Bedwind in Old English, indicates a place where wild clematis grew in great profusion.'

FROM AN AMERICAN WEB SITE DEVOTED TO GENEALOGY

It would be wholly appropriate were Great Bedwyn to be named after the clematis, an attractive plant that adds a splash of colour to many of the local properties. Great Bedwyn is a fine village – indeed, from the 11th century until 1832 it was actually a market town with borough status. This was an archetypal rotten borough, too, a settlement of some 1,060 persons that managed to return two members to Westminster! It still manages to exude the qualities of a small town, with its rows of brick cottages and a scattering of handsome town houses, often set back or slightly to one side.

Great Bedwyn has a long tradition of stone masonry, associated with the Lloyd family whose premises (*inset*) are located in Church Street opposite St Mary the Virgin church. The Lloyd family came to Great Bedwyn to work on the construction of the Kennet & Avon Canal back in the early 19th century, with one Benjamin Lloyd being employed on the construction of the nearby Bruce Tunnel in 1803. The Church Street premises are open to the public as a Stone Museum, and contain such exhibits as restored and painted texts, fonts, statuary and mounted fossils. Opposite the museum, St Mary's church houses an effigy of Sir John Seymour, whose daughter married Henry VIII in 1536.

To the west of Bedwyn at Crofton lies the summit of the Kennet & Avon Canal. There were inevitable water supply problems on this section of the canal as water flowed downhill through the waterway's lock chambers. The solution was to construct a reservoir – Wilcot

Water - by damming a local stream. Water was pumped from the reservoir along Crofton Leat, a small artificial channel, into Crofton Top Lock. A pair of Cornish beam engines were installed in the pump house at Crofton (*opposite*) and, following their restoration in 1970, these are believed to be the oldest operational steam engines in the world.

THE KENNET & AVON CANAL

'The guns were fired on Sydney Wharf to announce the completion of work on the Kennet and Avon Canal.'

Bath Herald, 1810

When canal mania gripped Britain in the late 18th century, it did not go unnoticed even in the normally sedate West Country. A simple advertisement in a Salisbury journal in 1792, announcing a meeting in Devizes to discuss a proposed waterway to Bristol, caused businessmen from that city to head into the depths of the Wiltshire countryside.

There was clearly no shortage of venture capital, attracted by the high returns that investors had earned on such investments elsewhere in Britain. A line was surveyed by the engineer, John Rennie, royal assent was granted in 1784, and in the same year work began on the Kennet & Avon Canal. The River Kennet between Newbury and Reading had been navigable since the early 18th century, as had the Avon Navigation between Bath and Bristol. All that remained was to bridge the gap between Bath and Newbury, a mere 57 miles, and London would have a direct waterway link with Bristol.

The greatest surprise to be found along the length of the waterway is on the western approaches to Devizes. Within a distance of little more than 2 miles, 29 locks were constructed to carry the Kennet & Avon Canal up an ascent of over 230 ft from the Avon Valley to the town's wharf. Sixteen of these locks come in quick succession as the canal makes its final ascent of Caen Hill (*inset*). It was the completion of the Caen Hill staircase in 1810 that marked the end of construction work on the canal and the firing of those guns in Bath.

Traffic on the canal followed an all too familiar pattern. There was an initial boom, with 341,878 tons of freight being carried in 1838, followed by a virtual collapse due to the stiff competition from the railways. By 1955, the K&A was listed as a Grade III waterway – 'a canal which is either disused or carries insufficient trade to justify its retention as a commercial waterway'. In the post-war years, the Kennet and Avon Canal Trust has worked closely with the British Waterways Board to breathe fresh life into this great waterway as here at Little Bedwyn (*opposite*).

BRADFORD-ON-AVON

'The excitement of Bradford-on-Avon is its position, with the hills rising steeply to the north, houses appearing on top of houses and steps connecting the streets.'

NIKOLAUS PEVSNER

Bradford-on-Avon's wealth was founded upon the woollen trade, with the mills being powered by the waters of the River Avon. Whilst the affluent mill-owners resided in grand town houses and country residences, the mill workers had to settle for humbler dwellings, many of which lie spread across the hillside above the river. The weavers' cottages, whose terraces are known as Newtown, Middle Rank and Tory, are only accessible on foot, a delight for residents but a serious problem for removal companies who charge a premium when conducting business in this part of the town.

Bradford-on-Avon was historically a 'broad ford' through the Avon. Since the 14th century, however, passing traffic has crossed the river by means of the handsome Town Bridge (*opposite*). Two of the original arches remain to this day, with the remaining arches dating back to the 17th century. In the middle of the bridge is a diminutive lock-up, which in days gone by housed prisoners *en route* to gaols in Bristol and Bath. The prisoners would talk of being 'under the fish and over the water' on account of the fish-shaped weather vane above the lock-up.

Amongst Bradford's other architectural delights are a diminutive Saxon church (*inset*) and a hugely impressive tithe barn. The Saxon church of St Lawrence only came to light in 1856, when the local vicar looked out across the roof tops and noticed a mysterious cross. It is a plain building, as high as it is long, with very little by way of internal embellishment. In many ways, the beauty of the Saxon church lies in its very simplicity.

With so much to enjoy in what has been described as 'Bath in miniature', it is not difficult to see why Bradford-on-Avon featured in a BBC series focussing on ten of the best small towns in England.

DEVIZES

'Devizes, Devizes, full of surprises.'

A LOCAL SAYING

Devizes is one of the finest old market towns in the whole of the county. The spacious market place (*inset*) was historically the setting for a popular corn market, where a cautionary tale is told on the inscription on the Market Cross. It relates to Ruth Pierce, a maiden from one of the nearby villages who, when accused of not paying for a bag of wheat, told the trader that she wished to drop down dead were she to be found to be lying. On repeating this solemn

oath, she breathed her last and fell to the ground, her ill-gotten gain still in her hand.

Such is the stuff of legends, another of which relates to the Crammer, a pond on Devizes Green. It is here that visitors discover the story of the moonrakers – dealers in contraband, who stored their barrels of liquor on the bed of this pool of water. One evening, when caught by the local constabulary attempting to bring their contraband to the surface, they acted the part of simpletons. Pointing to the reflection of the moon in the water, they told the police officer that they were attempting to bring a supposed lump of precious metal to the surface!

Whilst on the subject of alcohol, Devizes is home to Wadworth's famous Northgate Brewery, a vast redbrick edifice that dominates the western end of the Market Place. Established in 1885 by Henry Wadworth, the brewery is best known for its 6X brew, although the seasonal 'Old Timer' is reckoned by real ale buffs to be the classic beer from this fine brewery.

To celebrate the new millennium, the Devizes-based sculptor, Eric Standford, was commissioned to create a Celtic cross. Carved from Portland stone, the twenty carved panels on the cross (*opposite*) illustrate themes that extend from local history and Christianity through to more general symbols such as the Four Seasons and the Four Ages of Man. Unveiled on a glorious summer's day by the town mayor, the Millennium Cross is a handsome addition to the architectural delights of St John's church.

WESTBURY AND EDINGTON

'As from the Dorset shore I travelled home,
I saw the charger of the Wiltshire wold;
A far-seen figure, stately to behold,
Whose groom the shepherd is, the hoe his comb.'

CHARLES TENNYSON TURNER (1808-1879)

Westbury rose to prominence as a railway town, lying at the halfway point on the mainline from London to the West Country. This was where engine crews were changed, and tenders refilled with coal, as the great expresses headed west to the resorts and beaches of Devon and Cornwall. Nowadays, many visitors head this way to visit the nearby white horse carved into the downland escarpment above the town (*opposite*).

The original horse, said to have been cut to commemorate King Alfred's victory over the Danes at the Battle of Ethandune in 878 AD, actually resembled a cart horse! In 1778, local records record how it was 'remodelled by a wretch named George Gee', a steward to Lord Abingdon. One can but speculate whether the name 'G Gee' had made him overly sensitive about horses.

Adjoining the white horse on this lofty vantage point is Bratton Castle, an Iron Age hillfort that overlooks the flat clay vale below. Constructed sometime between 300 BC and 43 AD, the ramparts enclose a site of some 25 acres, an enclosure that contains a distinctive long barrow. The views from the hillfort are quite exceptional – clearly no place could have been better adapted for a fortress.

Below Bratton Castle, nestling at the foot of the escarpment, lies Edington's priory church (*inset*). Nikolaus Pevsner described Edington church as being 'wonderful and highly important, so varied in its skyline and so freely embattled that it looks like a fortified mansion'. He was also impressed with 'the solemn lines of the downs rising immediately to the south that are a perfect foil'. This is praise indeed from one of England's harshest architectural critics.

WARMINSTER AND LONGLEAT

*'Nestling in the valley of the River Wylye, the town of Warminster presents an
image of England that seems ever stable and tranquil . . .'*

JOHN RIMMER, WARMINSTER REVISITED WEBSITE

It was in the Middle Ages that Warminster rose to prominence as a settlement. As with much of the West Country, the cloth and wool trade brought vast wealth to the town, which also became a noted corn market. Many of the fine buildings in the Market Place owe their origins to this era in the town's history, when they served as stores and warehouses, as well as inns and hostelries for traders who would travel great distances to conduct their business affairs in this thriving Wiltshire market town (*inset*).

The writer and historian William Cobbett passed this way back in 1826, and was mightily impressed with the quality of agriculture in the area. He described the surrounding farmland as being fertile and productive, as he discovered an agricultural base founded upon arable farming as well as the rearing of thousands of sheep. Cobbett recorded that this livestock production yielded 'beautiful meat – the best I have seen anywhere' whilst he commented that the town of Warminster was both 'solid and good'.

Today, it is nearby Longleat that attracts most tourists to the area. Following the destruction of the original house by fire in 1567, Sir John Thynne spent twelve years supervising the construction of a magnificent new mansion, built in the then newly-popular Italian style (*opposite*). In the 18th century, 'Capability' Brown was employed to lay out the formal gardens, orangery and terrace, which he completed with his usual genius and total lack of concern for cost! In recent years, attractions such as a safari park and a giant maze have been added to the Longleat estate, to generate the funds necessary to maintain such a vast property in the 21st century.

STONEHENGE

'The stones are great and magic power they have
Men that are sick fare to that stone
And they wash that stone
And with that water bathe away their sickness'

LAYAMON, from the poem *Brut* (AD 1200)

There is no doubting the importance of this great prehistoric site. Dating from 2,800 BC, this was originally a simple henge monument consisting of a bank and external ditch. The concentric stone circles, a mixture of sarsens from the Marlborough Downs and bluestones from the Prescelly Mountains in West Wales, were a later addition. Almost certainly some sort of sacred site for ancient man, speculation remains as to its precise function.

In the fields around the stones lie a collection of other ancient monuments that includes two fine groups of barrows, as well as the Avenue, a ceremonial walkway that would have provided a splendid approach to Stonehenge during ancient religious rituals. There is also the Cursus, whose precise function is as puzzling as that of the ancient stones. A remarkable enclosure consisting of two parallel banks and ditches, 100 yards apart and 1½ miles in length, it has even been suggested that this was the site of both horse and chariot racing.

Whilst it is easy for the cynic to dismiss Stonehenge as yet another example of 'Theme Park Britain', there can be no doubting the impressiveness of this site. When viewed from one of the ancient tracks that cross this corner of Salisbury Plain, away from the inevitable trappings of mass tourism, the monument really does come to life. Witness the stones emerging from early morning mist, or fading into an autumnal sunset, and you will certainly have cast your eyes on one of the wonders of this world.

THE DEVERILLS

*'Across the meadow, farms project a night
of shadow over yarrow mint.
The stream's eclipsed; you only hear its voice:
The birds have sung.'*

●

NICK HANCOCK, from *An Ash Tree Liturgy*

Nick Hancock's poem was influenced by the River Wylye and its majestic course through the downland of South Wiltshire (*opposite*). Follow the river upstream from its confluence with the Avon near Salisbury Cathedral, and your journey will initially take you to Warminster, by way of historic Wilton and the Codfords.

Above Warminster, this chalk stream swings in a south-easterly

direction to add beauty and delight to the Deverills – Kingston Deverill, Monkton Deverill, Brixton Deverill and Longbridge Deverill – a series of villages set against a backdrop of some of the county's finest downland.

The name 'Deverill' could not be more apt as a description of the valley and its scenery. The first part of the name can be traced back to 'Dubro' – a British word for 'water' – whilst the ending is derived from 'ial' – meaning a 'cultivated upland region'.

The hilltops above Brixton Deverill have been cultivated since time immemorial. Here we find Cold Kitchen Hill, the name implying 'meatless bones'. Certainly, an extensive Romano-Celtic temple was unearthed on this lofty hilltop site, an archaeological relic that also housed a cremation area. Proof of this were the partially burnt brooches found during excavations, clear evidence – according to the archaeologists – of a crematorium.

Downstream lies Longbridge Deverill (*inset*), the largest of the Deverill villages. The oldest part of the village is at its northern end, where the Thynne Almshouses – named after Sir James Thynne of Longleat – lie alongside St Paul's church, the grouping standing just above the Wylye.

In this corner of the Wylye valley we find John Hurd, one of the few growers of organic cress in the country. His 47 beds are fed every day with three million gallons of pure spring water pumped up from bore holes 120 ft down in the chalk. It is this pure water that also makes the Wylye a much-loved river, especially amongst fly fishermen whose prize trout flourish in such perfect conditions.

WYLYE

'A person by the name of Popjay, of mean extraction, went abroad in his early youth, and after some years returned to Wily in his carriage, and with a show of having acquired considerable wealth, he caused this expensive tomb to be built . . .'

SIR RICHARD COLT HOARE, *History of Wiltshire* (1825)

Wylye is indeed the sort of place that one might wish to return to following travels around the globe and the acquisition of much wealth. With street names such as 'Sheepwash Lane' and Teapot Street', and with the River Wylye running quietly beneath an ancient stone bridge, the setting overlooked by a nearby mill house, the village is the archetypal English settlement.

The oldest part of the village – and the most picturesque – can be found around the church and the Bell Inn, a hostelry whose origins can be traced back to the 14th century. This was a coaching stop for travellers *en route* from Bristol and Bath to Salisbury and the south coast, and its beams and timbering, stripped masonry and log fires, still lend the Bell a timeless feel.

Nearby Steeple Langford (*inset*) has an intriguing name! The consensus view appears to be that the name is derived from the wooden posts or 'staples' which marked the route of a long ford across the Wylye. An alternative view is that the name could come from 'staple', a term connected with wool production in the West of England.

Despite the intrusive presence of the A36 truck road, Steeple Langford still manages to exude a certain rural charm and detachment. Above the steepled church sits the local manor house, surrounded by damp meadowland and the River Wylye, whilst round about are dotted more humble dwellings, fashioned from the local flint and chalk. It is altogether a most beautiful corner of Olde England.

STOURHEAD

'Henry Hoare, a member of a London banking family, created at his Wiltshire home of Stourhead one of the finest landscape gardens to be seen anywhere in the world . . .'

AA PLACES TO VISIT IN GREAT BRITAIN (1988)

Henry Hoare I, a wealthy London banker, bought the Manor of Stourton in 1718, demolished the old Stourton House, and in its place erected an imposing Palladian mansion – Stourhead House. The

house contains a fine collection of art treasures, which include paintings by Gainsborough, Reynolds, Canaletto and Raphael, as well as some items of furniture constructed by Thomas Chippendale the younger, on the Stourhead premises.

The grandeur of the mansion is – if anything – overshadowed by the adjoining Stourhead Gardens, quite rightly ranked as one of the most famous landscaped gardens in the world. Henry Hoare II dammed springs of the River Stour to create a majestic lake, around which he placed classical temples, rustic grottos and bridges. It was an attempt to produce an imitation of the dreamy landscapes featured in the paintings of Claude Lorrain and Gaspar Poussin.

Whilst the layout of the garden still resembles Hoare's original creation, today the surrounding grounds include a number of trees and shrubs that would have been unknown to Hoare. Exotic clumps of azalea and rhododendron, for example, provide splashes of colour in May and June that would have been unrecognisable in the 18th century. Pathways meander around the grounds, from grottos with their statues of Nymph and River God to high vantage points - such as the Temple of Apollo - with its commanding view across the estate.

On the hilltop above Stourhead – and marking Wiltshire's border with Somerset – stands Alfred's Tower. The inscription on this 160 ft high brick construction suggests that this is the spot where Alfred rallied his troops before the victory over the Danes at Ethandune. Whether the tower marks the actual spot where *'there came unto him all the men of Somerset, and the Wiltshire men'* is a matter for some conjecture. It is perhaps more realistic to follow the line that the tower was built to mark peace with France and the succession of George III in 1760.

MERE AND MILTON

'An' birds do whissle over head,
An' water's bubblen in its bed,
An' there vor me the apple tree
Do lean down low in Linden Lea.'

———————•———————

WILLIAM BARNES, *My Orcha'd in Linden Lea*

Crafted of local stone, the town of Mere (*inset*) sits on the Wiltshire-Dorset border. Named after John Mere, it is the tower of St Michael's church that dominates the centre of the town, but even this landmark is overshadowed by nearby Castle Hill. The 13th-century castle, with its six towers, has sadly gone, having fallen into disrepair in the 15th century.

The good number of Georgian properties in the centre of Mere include The Chantry, at one time a school run by William Barnes, the noted Dorset poet. The town also enjoys royal connections, Charles II having rested in the George Hotel following his escape from the Battle of Worcester back in 1651. Amongst the other handsome features in Mere are the Old Ship Inn, with its unusual 18th-century iron sign, and an eye-catching clock tower.

The view from Castle Hill is well worth the climb. Extending over three counties – Wiltshire, Dorset and Somerset – a conveniently placed plinth sets out the various landmarks that are visible from this lofty hilltop perch. As well as the nearby Vale of Wardour, the outlook encompasses the flat clay vale of the Stour as well as Whitesheet Hill, a majestic stretch of chalk downland.

The villages around Mere are some of the most attractive and interesting in the county. East Knoyle, for example, is the birthplace of Sir Christopher Wren. A plaque records his achievements as an 'architect, mathematician and patriot'. Adjoining East Knoyle is the hamlet of Milton (*opposite*), a quintessentially English settlement.

Handsome cottages and rambling houses line a peaceful country lane, set against a backdrop of woodland and pasture.

In this simplicity – and lack of ostentation – lies the beauty of these off-the-beaten-track settlements. This is the essence of a rapidly fading English charm.

THE TEFFONTS

'A pretty village by a little stream.'

Nikolaus Pevsner (1963)

In 1934, the neighbouring villages of Teffont Magna and Teffont Evias, deep in the South Wiltshire countryside (*opposite*), were officially combined to form the parish of Teffont. These are picture-book settlements of great charm, quite rightly described by one commentator as 'chocolate box villages'. Any commercial venture looking for images for a calendar or greetings card, a biscuit tin or a fudge box, need look no further!

Both villages contain a scattering of 17th and 18th-century cottages, constructed of Purbeck stone, with the ancient Black Horse Inn standing between the two settlements. Emerging from the local chalk hills is the Teff, a small stream that runs through the Teffonts – where it is crossed by a series of small stone bridges – on the way to its confluence with the River Nadder. It is, to quote a local guidebook, 'a setting of pure English beauty and tranquillity'.

In Teffont Evias, we find St Michael and All Angels church, whose 125 ft spire stands aloft the village's cottages and houses. John Mayne, the Lord of the Manor, whose grand residence stands alongside St Michael's and All Angels, largely rebuilt the church in 1821. The Manor House, with its four-bayed frontage, battlements and towered Victorian outbuildings, dates from the early 17th century.

In Teffont Magna (*inset*), St Edward's church is on an altogether different scale. Tiny and chapel like, this is an older place of worship, dating from the 13th century. Interestingly enough, neither church had a dedication until the Bishop of Sherborne intervened in 1965. St Edward was one of the dedications of the Abbey of Shaftesbury, with which Teffont had been associated through the charter of AD 871 in which King Alfred gave the village to the Abbess.

In the words of local estate agents, both Teffont Magna and Teffont Evias are 'much sought after villages'. With their handsome thatched cottages fronting onto the Teff, where the occasional kingfisher adds colour to the scene, it is not hard to see why. This is a truly beautiful corner of a most beautiful county.

SALISBURY

'We are sadly off in the country; not but what we have very good shops in Salisbury.'

JANE AUSTEN, *Northanger Abbey*

Old Sarum, the original site of Salisbury, was abandoned by Bishop Poore in 1220. Constant disagreements between the down-to-earth soldiers in the castle and the spiritual bishopric led to the Christian brothers laying the foundations of a new cathedral a mile or two to the south. This was New Sarum, the roots of modern day Salisbury. The town was built on a grid system of six streets running west to east, crossed by five running north to south, with each square of streets being named after some prominent building.

Henry III granted Salisbury's first charter in 1227, with later charters extending the range of the city's rights and privileges. The city had always been a flourishing market centre, with many craft guilds being established in medieval times. Butcher Row and Ox Row, Blue Boar Row and Salt Lane date from this period in Salisbury's history, as does the occasional mill along the rivers Avon and Nadder. Originally corn mills, these later became fulling mills associated with cloth production.

Many of the fine buildings in the city date from this era, too. The 15th-century Poultry Cross, the last remaining market cross, stands at the junction of Silver and Minster Streets, opposite the 14th-century Haunch of Venison and other timber-framed properties. Butcher Row is lined with gabled medieval houses, whilst in New Canal – named after the open streams that once ran through the streets – stands the house of John Halle. Built between 1470 and 1485, this wool-merchant's residence boasts a splendid timber roof of six bays.

Queen Street (*opposite*) is equally impressive. From red-brick Georgian houses through to 15th-century, timber-framed, overhanging properties, there is something to catch the eye at every turn. It truly is one of the great historic centres in Britain and, after Winchester, the second city of the ancient kingdom of Wessex.

SALISBURY

'Rare example of an English Gothic church built entirely to one basic design. Internal storeys clearly separated into strong horizontal bands; extensive use of Purbeck marble to create a strong coloured scheme.'

SIR BANISTER FLETCHER, *A History of Architecture*

From whichever direction the visitor approaches Salisbury, there is one landmark that never fails to catch the eye – the spire of Salisbury Cathedral. Generations of schoolchildren, with their well-thumbed copies of the *Guinness Book of Records*, could tell you that at 404 ft, this is the tallest spire in the country. What is less well known is the fact that this handsome edifice is set upon foundations a mere 5 to 6 ft deep, foundations that lie on the wet ground of the River Avon's water meadows and yet support an ancient monument weighing some 6,400 tonnes!

This potential instability has left the cathedral subject to structural stress over the centuries. When Sir Christopher Wren surveyed the spire in 1668, he found it to be some 30 inches out of plumb. Iron tie-rods were inserted to brace the spire and, when removed some 200 years later, measurement revealed that no further movement had occurred. Such was the genius of Wren.

The great beauty of Salisbury Cathedral – as recorded by Sir Banister Fletcher – is its uniform design. The cathedral was begun in 1220, when Bishop Poore decided that keeping the company of military men at Old Sarum was too troublesome, with most of the building work having been completed by 1258. Unlike most British cathedrals that have evolved over the centuries, Salisbury's completion in just a single generation is unique.

The architecture is an absolute delight. Ancient tradition maintained that there were as many pillars in and around the cathedral as there are hours in the year, and as many windows as there were days in the year. Whether or not there is any truth in this legend, the setting above the water meadows of the River Avon (*opposite*) – as well as the neighbouring Close whose green spaces are surrounded by fine period houses – is an absolute delight.

THE ARMY

'Seven miles from any town
There stands Imber on the Down.'

AN OLD RHYME

Salisbury Plain has been a military training ground for over 100 years, the land being purchased by the armed forces as far back as 1897. The first permanent barracks were established at Tidworth in 1905, at which time the War Department had some 43,000 acres of land at its disposal. In 1920, the Larkhill School of Artillery was built, with the Warminster Infantry Training Centre dating from 1937.

Today's statistics are even more impressive. At 93,000 acres, the

Salisbury Plain Training Area is the largest military training area in the UK, with the military training garrisons at Bulford, Larkhill, Tidworth and Warminster containing 14,000 soldiers. Some 600,000 man-days are spent in training on the Plain each year, with over 9 million large-calibre rounds having been fired during the last 35 years.

Not everyone is enamoured with the Army's presence on the Plain, however. On 1st November 1943, the villagers of Imber – a remote settlement in the heart of Salisbury Plain (*inset*) – were given until 17th December to leave their homes and farms to allow the entire area to be used by US troops. Despite villagers assuming this was a temporary move, they were never allowed to return to their homes. Such was the sadness amongst the community that the village blacksmith is said to have died of a broken heart.

Once a year, on the Saturday nearest to the feast of St Giles, a service is still held in Imber church, where the few surviving villagers, their relatives and the mere curious cross the Plain to this isolated hamlet.

On a more positive note, the Army's presence on the Plain has prevented this wilderness area from the ravages of modern development. Some 2,300 ancient monuments, 6,000 acres of woodland and a wealth of rare flora and fauna exist on Salisbury Plain. It is a truly remote and undisturbed landscape, as is so obvious to the thousands of visitors who cross the Plain's byways on the occasional bank holiday when the public are granted access rights.

OLD SARUM AND WILTON

'This is a significant place in the history of Parliamentary democracy (or lack of it).'

JOHN CHANDLER, *Footsteps* (2002)

Old Sarum, a prime hilltop site, is one of those pieces of real estate that has long attracted the interest of every conceivable wave of invader and settler. The massive ramparts and ditches (*opposite*) were constructed during the Iron Age, and subsequently the Romans, the Saxons, the Danes and the Normans each, in turn, occupied the site and left their mark. For the Romans, this was an important staging point at the junction of five roads. Sorviodunum – to give Old Sarum its Roman name – lay at the hub of highways running to Badbury Rings and Dorchester, the lead mines in the Mendips, Silchester, Winchester and Mildenhall.

Old Sarum became a Saxon burgh which was given military and ecclesiastical importance by the Normans to the extent that, at the start of the medieval period, the hill-fort had become the basis of a town with a castle, cathedral and many houses. The soldiers proved to be such disagreeable neighbours for the clergy, however, that in 1331 the cathedral was abandoned. Its materials were moved to the site of 'New Sarum' – modern Salisbury – where it was rebuilt.

In nearby Wilton, the ancient capital of Wessex, stands the Wilton Carpet Factory (*inset*). This world-renowned business can trace its origins to a humble French carpet weaver, brought to England by the Earl of Pembroke to pass on his skills to the local weavers. In 1835, handlooms from the bankrupt Axminster factory in Devon were moved here and hand-knotted Axminster carpets were manufactured alongside traditional Wilton carpets. Over the years, Wilton carpets have adorned both royal and presidential palaces, as well as some of the world's grandest hotels and cruise liners.

TROWBRIDGE

*'On a small stone bridge over the Biss at Trowbridge stands a building of perforated brickwork,
the only local example left of a handle house. In this, teazles, damp from use on
the wet cloth, were dried by a current of air.'*

M.C. CORFIELD, *The Industrial Archaeology of Wiltshire* (1978)

Trowbridge (*opposite*) does seem rather an odd choice for the county town of Wiltshire. Neither as large as Swindon nor as historic as Salisbury, it was a fortuitous set of circumstances that led to the town becoming the administrative centre of the county.

Swindon and Salisbury were the obvious choices but there was no direct rail connection between the two, Salisbury Plain forming a natural barrier. Both towns, however, enjoyed a direct rail link with Trowbridge – hence its choice as county town.

Originally a centre for the local cloth trade, the town had become Wiltshire's largest weaving centre by the 14th century. Subsequently, profits from the trade financed the fine Georgian houses in the Parade, Fore Street and Roundstone Street, where the stone frontages of the merchants' houses are most impressive.

With the advent of power looms, many cloth workers faced redundancy. Factory buildings were burnt during the ensuing riots, with the alleged leader – Thomas Helliker – being executed on his 19th birthday in 1803. His tomb can be found in the local churchyard.

The last mill closed in the 1980s – as has Ushers Brewery in more recent times – but manufacturing industry still survives in the town. Bowyers, purveyors of fine meat products, operate out of town centre premises, whilst Airsprung Beds thrive and prosper on one of the town's industrial estates.

The remains of the textile trade lie scattered around the town, most unusually in the shape of Handel's House. This was where teazels were hung to dry after being used to 'brush' the locally produced wool.

OLD WARDOUR CASTLE

'The fascination of these ruins is increased by the romantic gardens laid out by Lord Arundell, complete with cedars, a Gothic garden house and grottoes by the Wiltshire grotto builder John Lane.'

GEOFFREY GRIGSON, *Wessex* (1951)

Many years ago, I was following a remote footpath through the depths of rural South Wiltshire when I stumbled across a most surprising site. Below a belt of woodland, in quite splendid isolation, stood this ruinous fortress, the archetypal romantic relic – this was Old Wardour Castle (*opposite*).

Whilst today we imagine castles to be powerful fortresses, back in the 14th century, it had become extremely fashionable to build a castle with comfortable accommodation that could be used for lavish entertainment. Thus, it was in 1393 that Lord Lovel, a veteran of the Hundred Years War, was granted a licence to crenellate his residence to create the perfect retirement home.

Lovel's family remained at Old Wardour for only 60 years until, on the accession of Edward IV, as Lancastrians, they forfeited the property. The castle passed through a succession of owners until in 1570 it was purchased by Sir Matthew Arudell. Together with the architect Robert Smythson, whose previous contracts had included work on Longleat House, a major reconstruction resulted in a property that was a combination of the

Renaissance imposed on the Gothic tradition.

The Arundell family were Royalists and, in 1643, the Parliamentary leader Sir Thomas Hungerford besieged the castle. The Roundheads took the property, but six months later Sir Matthew's son returned to retrieve the family home. To cut a long story short, the castle was ruined beyond repair, with the Arundell family eventually building a smaller residence on the south side of the outer wall.

In 1756, a scheme was put forward to reconstruct the castle, but this was rejected. The then Lord Arundell built a new house of vast proportions to the north-west – now known as Wardour Castle – whose formal gardens were laid out to contain the ruins of what became known as Old Wardour Castle. Old Wardour became a true romantic relic, lying in a gentle state of decay, only to rise to national acclaim during the filming of *Robin Hood – Prince of Thieves*.